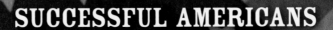

SUCCESSFUL AMERICANS

Korean Americans

Gail Snyder

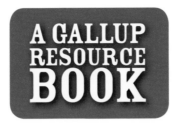

A GALLUP
RESOURCE
BOOK

Mason Crest Publishers
Philadelphia

Produced by OTTN Publishing in association with
Bow Publications, Inc.

MASON CREST PUBLISHERS INC.
370 Reed Road
Broomall, Pennsylvania 19008
(866) MCP-BOOK (toll free)
www.masoncrest.com

Printed in the United States of America.

First Printing

9 8 7 6 5 4 3 2 1

Library of Congress Cataloging-in-Publication Data

Snyder, Gail.
  Korean Americans / Gail Snyder.
     p. cm. — (Successful Americans)
  Includes bibliographical references.
  ISBN: 978-1-4222-0518-1 (hardcover)
  ISBN: 978-1-4222-0864-9 (pbk.)
 1. Korean Americans—Juvenile literature. 2. Korean Americans—Biography—Juvenile literature. 3. Korean Americans—Social conditions—Juvenile literature. I. Title.
  E184.K6S59 2008
  973'.04957—dc22
                                                    2008029821

Publisher's note:
All quotations in this book come from original sources, and contain the spelling and grammatical inconsistencies of the original text.

◀ **CROSS-CURRENTS** ▶

When you see this logo, turn to the Cross-Currents section at the back of the book. The Cross-Currents features explore connections between people, places, events, and ideas.

Table of Contents

Korean-American children wave U.S. flags during a rally in the Los Angeles community of Koreatown. More than 1.4 million people of Korean ancestry live in the United States today.

CHAPTER ONE

Two Koreas

During the first decades of the 20th century, there were few Korean immigrants living on the mainland of the United States. By 1940 the number had reached only about 2,000. But during the second half of the century, the number of Korean Americans grew significantly. Today, according to the 2005 American Community Survey of the U.S. Census Bureau, there are more than 1.4 million Americans of Korean ancestry living in the United States.

EARLY IMMIGRATION

Korean civilization dates back some 4,000 years, but throughout its history the region has often been dominated by its neighbors. During the 1600s the Chinese ruled the Korean peninsula. In 1895, when the Japanese defeated the Chinese in the Sino-Japanese War, the Koreans briefly enjoyed 15 years of independence. But in 1910 Japan annexed Korea, making it a Japanese province and outlawing the Korean language and culture.

During the Japanese occupation few Koreans traveled to the United States—they were forbidden by the Japanese from emigrating. But even before the occupation there had been little migration to America. With the exception of a handful of students and traders, Koreans did not arrive in U.S. territory until January 1903, when 102 men, women, and children aboard the *S.S. Gaelic* landed in Hawaii to work on the island's sugar plantations. During this initial wave of immigration, which ended around 1905, around 8,000 Korean workers came to Hawaii. About a thousand of them eventually made their way to the mainland of the United States, most arriving at San Francisco, California.

The number of Koreans coming to the United States was severely curtailed in the 1920s, when the U.S. Congress passed a series of anti-immigration measures that limited the number of Asians permitted to enter the country. In 1924 Congress designated Asia as a "barred zone" from which immigration was totally prohibited. Still, some 300 Korean students managed to enter the United States between 1925 and 1940. By 1940 there were just 2,000 Korean immigrants, most of whom were farm workers, living on the American mainland.

TWO KOREAS

After the Second World War (1939–1945), growing tensions between the United States and the Soviet Union, known as the cold war, led to the division in 1948 of Korea into two countries separated at the 38ᵗʰ parallel. The communist government of the Soviet Union supported the Democratic People's Republic of Korea, or North Korea. It was ruled by Kim Il-sung from the capital city of Pyongyang. Western nations supported the Republic of Korea, or South Korea. Anti-communist leader Syngman Rhee served as the first president of South Korea, which had its capital in Seoul.

Two years later, in 1950, North Korean troops, assisted by the Chinese and armed by the Soviets, flooded across the border in an effort to unify Korea under communist rule. The North Korean army was repelled by an American-led coalition of United Nations troops. The Korean War raged for three years, until a ceasefire was declared on July 23, 1953. Almost 3 million Koreans died or were wounded during the war, and millions were left homeless and separated from family members. More than 35,000 Americans lost their lives in the conflict.

Since the 1953 truce North Korea and South Korea have maintained an uneasy peace, and troops remain on alert on both sides of the border. The two Koreas have developed separate

The Korean peninsula, in East Asia, contains the Democratic People's Republic of Korea in the north and the Republic of Korea in the south.

societies, economies, and cultures. South Korea and Western nations remain wary of North Korean dictator Kim Jong Il because of his country's development of nuclear weapons.

IMMMIGRATION AFTER THE WAR

In 1952 Congress passed the McCarran-Walter Act, which lifted prohibitions against Asian immigration. However, quotas of only 100 visas per year for each Asian nation restricted the

Concerns about the country's military and weapons capabilities have affected how Americans view North Korea. As a 2008 Gallup poll showed, most Americans have an unfavorable opinion. On the other hand, a large percentage of Americans have a favorable attitude toward South Korea, which is the homeland of the majority of Korean Americans:

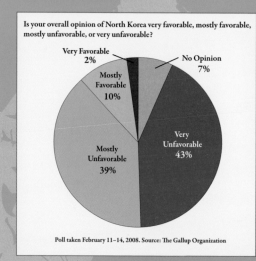

Is your overall opinion of North Korea very favorable, mostly favorable, mostly unfavorable, or very unfavorable?

Very Favorable 2%
Mostly Favorable 10%
No Opinion 7%
Very Unfavorable 43%
Mostly Unfavorable 39%

Poll taken February 11–14, 2008. Source: The Gallup Organization

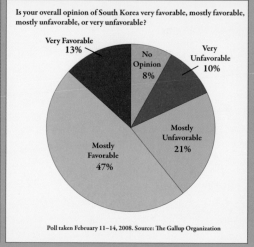

Is your overall opinion of South Korea very favorable, mostly favorable, mostly unfavorable, or very unfavorable?

Very Favorable 13%
No Opinion 8%
Very Unfavorable 10%
Mostly Unfavorable 21%
Mostly Favorable 47%

Poll taken February 11–14, 2008. Source: The Gallup Organization

number of Koreans allowed into the country. The law did give Asians the right to seek U.S. citizenship—which had been illegal since the 1920s. During the 1950s some South Koreans immigrated to the United States, seeking economical or educational opportunities. But U.S. immigration quotas kept their numbers low. Emigration from North Korea was not allowed.

The Korean War brought about an increase in immigration, but not by students or professional workers. About 500,000 American troops served during the war, and tens of thousands were stationed in Korea after the ceasefire was signed. Many American soldiers married Korean women, and returned home with them. Between 1950 and 1965, more than 15,000 Koreans immigrated to the United States. Around 40 percent of them were war brides, who obtained citizenship because of their marriage to a U.S. citizen.

Adopted orphans were also part of Korean immigration. Some American servicemen fathered children with Korean women whom they did not marry. Because Korean society did not accept these mixed-race children, referred to as Amerasians, they were often abandoned by their mothers. Some children were taken in by orphanages, while others were left to fend for themselves on the streets.

Beginning in the 1950s some Amerasian children, as well as full-blooded Korean orphans, found homes with adoptive parents in the United States through American charities. One of these organizations, the Welcome House Adoption Program, was established by Pearl S. Buck, the Nobel Prize–winning American author who often wrote about life in the Asian world. Buck's organization and other charities were instrumental in finding homes in the United States for more than 100,000 children from South Korea.

RAPID GROWTH

In 1965 changes in U.S. immigration law had a significant impact on the number of Koreans entering the United States. That year Congress passed the Immigration and Nationality Act, which liberalized the quota system, raising the cap to as many as 20,000 visas per country. Priorities were given to immigrants with family members already in the United States, as well as to professionals. Refugees were also given priority status. The new law provided an opening for hundreds of thousands of Koreans to immigrate to the United States. Many of them were students who came to study at American universities and stayed after obtaining jobs.

Koreans became one of the fastest-growing immigrant groups in the United States. In just five years the estimated number of Koreans living in the United States doubled from 25,000 in 1965 to 50,000 in 1970. Ten years later, there were more than 350,000; by 1990 more than a million Koreans lived in the country.

Since first coming to the United States, when they were not allowed basic rights such as land ownership or citizenship, Koreans have dealt with anti-Asian prejudice. Some Korean owners of small businesses operating in low-income urban areas have also encountered hostility from other minority groups. In April 1992, vandals and looters destroyed thousands of Korean-owned businesses in south central Los Angeles during riots sparked by the police beating of an African American, Rodney King. The riots led Korean Americans in the L.A. community to organize politically to find ways to work in cooperation with other minority groups in their community.

◀ CROSS-CURRENTS ▶

To see how Americans' opinions on overall immigration to the United States have changed over the years, turn to page 50.

LIFE IN THE UNITED STATES

Today, the largest concentrations of Korean Americans are in the metropolitan regions of Los Angeles, California, and New York City (including northern New Jersey and southwestern Connecticut). Other significant populations can be found in and around Washington, D.C.; Augusta, Georgia; and El Paso, Texas. Many cities, including Los Angeles; New York; Chicago, Illinois; and Atlanta, Georgia have sections referred to as Koreatowns, which contain significant Korean-American populations.

Some Korean Americans are university educated, working in professional occupations as engineers, nurses, pharmacists, physicians, research scientists, professors, and corporate executives. Others are self-employed entrepreneurs operating their own businesses, including grocery stores, dry cleaners, gas stations, and other businesses. Yoon Cho, the owner of a shoe repair store in Augusta, Georgia, explains what draws many immigrants to the United States: "I love America," he says, "because if you work hard, the opportunities are there. Even if you don't have a lot of education, you can make money here. We are all equal."

The following chapters contain biographies of contemporary Korean Americans who have come to the United States or who are descended from Korean immigrants. Their contributions in fields such as medicine, literature, music, sports, and entertainment have added to U.S. society and helped ensure the country's prosperity.

CHAPTER TWO

Jim Yong Kim: World Leader in Medicine

Jim Yong Kim is a professor of medicine and chair of social medicine at Harvard Medical School, in Boston, Massachusetts. The Ivy League-trained physician and public health activist specializes in tuberculosis (TB), human immunodeficiency virus (HIV), and acquired immune deficiency syndrome (AIDS). He is also a cofounder of the Boston, Massachusetts-based nonprofit medical organization Partners in Health. The charitable organization coordinates medical programs to make modern, quality health care available for the poor around the world.

MUSCATINE, IOWA

Jim Yong Kim was born in Seoul, South Korea, on December 8, 1959. In search of greater economic opportunities, his father, Nhak Hee Kim, a dentist, moved the family to the United States. The Kims arrived in Iowa in 1964, when Jim was five years old. After first settling in State Center, a town of only 2,000 residents, they moved again to the larger town of Muscatine.

Muscatine is located near Iowa City, home of the University of Iowa. The Kims moved there so Jim's mother, Oaksook Chun, would have an easy commute to the university, where she was a doctoral candidate. There were just two

Jim Yong Kim is a renowned physician, university professor, and leader in global health and social medicine.

Asian families in Muscatine, including Jim's. At Muscatine High School Jim was the football team quarterback and starting guard on the basketball team. He graduated in 1978, distinguishing himself as class valedictorian.

From an early age Jim wanted to be a doctor and help others. Growing up, he was struck by the stories of poverty and destruction he saw on the television news, and he would talk with his mother about events that were happening in other places in the world. He was further inspired by lectures on international issues that he attended at the University of Iowa. Of particular interest were talks by Harvard Medical School psychologist Robert Coles and Vietnam War opponent William Sloane Coffin. Kim told an interviewer, "[The lectures] made me want to get out and see the world and to pursue the values I had learned."

PARTNERS IN HEALTH

After graduating from high school, Kim attended the University of Iowa. He later transferred to Brown University, in Providence, Rhode Island, where he received his bachelor's degree. He earned his medical degree from Harvard Medical School in 1991. Two years later he also earned a Ph.D. in medical anthropology from Harvard University.

While at Harvard, Kim established a strong friendship with Paul Farmer, a fellow student who shared a similar worldview

Steven Hilton, left, chairman and CEO of the Hilton Foundation, honors cofounders of Partners in Health (from left to right) Paul Farmer, Ophelia Dahl, and Jim Yong Kim, with the 2005 Hilton Humanitarian Prize. PIH was established in 1987 to provide worldwide health care for the poor.

about helping others. In 1983, just after being accepted to Harvard Medical School, Farmer had traveled to an impoverished village in central Haiti to provide health care. In 1987 Farmer, Kim, and several others cofounded the nonprofit group Partners in Health to establish and support clinics, other community health programs, and schools in central Haiti.

Farmer and Kim focused on developing effective methods of treating multi-drug resistant tuberculosis. A disease is said to be drug-resistant when the medication previously used to treat the illness no longer works. Drug-resistant strains can develop when the drug is not taken properly—for example, at the prescribed times or for the full course of treatment. Shortages of medicines in poor countries have led to incomplete TB treatments—and the development of multi-drug resistant tuberculosis around the world.

PIH helped launch a new TB-treatment program in which a variety of drugs to combat the disease are administered under supervision. Kim also successfully worked with U.S. and foreign pharmaceutical companies to reduce drug costs. In the past, the high cost of treatment typically meant that poor patients with tuberculosis would die. With the new system, however, cure rates improved dramatically.

◀ **CROSS-CURRENTS** ▶

For more information about Partners in Health and its cofounder Paul Farmer, turn to page 51.

MACARTHUR "GENIUS" FELLOWSHIP

In October 2003 Jim Kim won a MacArthur Fellowship, also known as the "genius award," which included a $500,000 cash prize (to be used as the recipient sees fit). The MacArthur Foundation praised Kim for a vision that inspired collaboration among local communities, world health organizations, political leaders, and pharmaceutical companies.

In thinking of how to spend the prize money, Kim commented to an interviewer, "It's a huge responsibility. It would be difficult to keep much for myself." He went on, "I want to find a way to accelerate what I've been doing for the past 15 [to] 20 years, helping the poor get access to better health care. Perhaps I can do something really significant. I feel a deep sense of responsibility to do so."

WORLD HEALTH LEADER

The success of PIH in treating drug-resistant tuberculosis brought Jim Yong Kim to the attention of the World Health Organization (WHO), a specialized agency of the United Nations that directs and coordinates health programs worldwide. Soon after receiving the MacArthur Genius Grant, Jim Kim took a leave of absence from Harvard and went to work for the

World Health Organization in Geneva, Switzerland, as senior adviser to WHO director-general Lee Jong-Wook.

In early 2004 Kim was appointed WHO HIV/AIDS director. In this position he oversaw WHO initiatives being established to help developing countries reach more people with HIV/AIDS treatment, prevention, and care programs.

A major program that Kim oversaw was the 3 x 5 initiative, an effort to provide 3 million people in developing countries with antiretrovirals (life-prolonging AIDS medication) by the end of 2005. When the 3 x 5 initiative began in 2003, only 300,000 AIDS patients in developing countries were receiving treatment.

As HIV/AIDS director at the UN's World Health Organization, Kim was part of the effort to increase the number of people in developing countries receiving the medications necessary to treat HIV/AIDS.

By the deadline of 2005, the initiative had significantly increased the number of new patients with access to medications to more than 1 million.

Kim was recognized for his work with the World Health Organization when he was named one of America's 25 best leaders by *U.S. News and World Report* in 2005. The following year he was named one of the 100 most influential people by *Time* magazine.

GLOBAL HEALTH

In addition to his work with Partners in Health, Kim teaches at the Harvard School of Public Health, where he is the François-Xavier Bagnoud (FXB) Professor of Health and Human Rights. He is also a professor of medicine at Harvard Medical School.

In a 2007 interview with *Harvard International Review*, Kim commented that he feels optimistic about the future of global health because of the commitment he see in the students he teaches. He noted that this attitude differed from when he was in medical school in the 1980s. "[O]nly a handful of my fellow students had an interest in the health of the poor and marginalized people in other countries," he wrote. But he was optimistic that today many more medical students were concerned with world health problems. "[M]ore than one-fourth of [the] first-year class has either had experience in or is interested in a career in global health. I have said on many occasions that our response to the problems of global health will define our generation."

CHAPTER THREE

Linda Sue Park: Author

Award-winning children's book author Linda Sue Park has written many stories that familiarize young people with Korean history, culture, and folklore, filling an important gap in literature that existed when she was growing up in the 1960s. Park is the first Korean American to win the Newbery Medal, a prestigious award given by the American Library Association to the author of the most distinguished contribution to American literature for children.

EARLY YEARS

Linda Sue Park was born March 25, 1960, in Urbana, Illinois, to Eung Won Ed, a civil engineer and computer programmer, and to Susie Kim, a teacher. Both parents were natives of South Korea who had come to the United States in the 1950s.

The oldest of three children, Linda Sue grew up in a home outside Chicago. Hers was an Americanized household—her mother and father spoke English at home. They did not teach Linda Sue how to speak Korean, and they did not take her to see their homeland until she was 12 years old.

READING AND WRITING

Reading was important to the Park family. Susie Kim taught her daughter to read when the girl was just four years old. Her father took her to the library every two weeks to check out new books. Linda Sue loved accompanying her father to the library, where she would lose herself in the fictionalized worlds of authors such as Laura Ingalls Wilder, who wrote the Little House series, and Frances Carpenter, who wrote *Tales of a Korean Grandmother*.

Park told an interviewer that she found it easy to go from being a reader to a writer: "I was a huge reader," she explained, "and I think that the gap, the jump from reading to writing never felt like a huge one. Because I loved reading so much, it seemed logical to try writing as well."

As a young child Linda Sue enjoyed writing poetry and short stories. She sold her first poem for one dollar when she was only four years old. The first publisher to recognize her budding talent was the children's magazine *Trailblazer*, which in 1969 purchased and published a haiku verse she had written. That first sale resulted in a check that her father thought important enough to frame. It was followed by other submissions to children's magazines that published her poetry as she was growing up.

Linda Sue Park has written numerous books that share stories of Korean history and culture with her readers.

WORKING WORLD

In 1981 Park graduated from Stanford University, in Palo Alto, California, with a bachelor of arts degree in English. But she did not begin her career as a creative writer. Instead she worked for an oil company, writing press releases and other corporate communications in its public relations department. She spent a few years in that job before moving to Dublin, Ireland, to join her boyfriend, Ben Dobbin, an Irish journalist she had met in the United States.

Ben and Linda Sue married in September 1984. The couple lived for several years in London, England, where their children Sean and Anna were born. During that time Park obtained a master's degree from Birkbeck College, worked at an advertising agency, and taught English to foreign students. She also wrote as a food and restaurant critic for a newspaper. In 1990 her husband's job took the family to New York State, first to Brooklyn (a borough of New York City) and later, Rochester. Park found work teaching English as a Second Language and wrote poetry published in literary magazines.

◄ CROSS-CURRENTS ►

To learn more about Linda Sue Park's experiences with teaching English as a Second Language, as well as information about the program, turn to page 52.

As Sean and Anna were growing up, Linda Sue discovered that what she wanted to do most of all was write books for young people. Her husband, Ben, encouraged her to pursue this new dream. She decided to learn more about her Korean heritage by writing historical fiction based on Korea's past. She explains:

> I have been writing all my life, but only after I had children of my own did I feel the desire to explore my ethnic heritage through writing. The fascinating discoveries I made have resulted in several books for young people. I continue to write poetry and fiction for adults as well, but because books were so important to me during childhood, my work in children's literature holds special importance in my heart.

BOOK AUTHOR

Park's first book, published in 1999, was *Seesaw Girl*. It tells the story of 12-year-old girl of 17th-century Korea. Because she is of a noble family, she is not allowed to leave her home until she marries. Her only glimpse of the outside world is what she can see from her seesaw.

Seesaw Girl was followed in 2001 by *The Kite Fighters*, which is about two 15th-century Korean brothers who build kites together but who are also rivals in kite-fighting competitions. The sport of kite-fighting in Korea dates back for many centuries. In competitions, each kite flyer uses his or her kite to knock down all the other kites.

In 2001 Park published her third young adult book, *A Single Shard*. In the story, a poor 12th-century Korean orphan breaks a priceless vase and must pay back the artisan who made it by working for him. As the boy begins to learn the art of ceramics, he becomes determined to become a potter himself.

A Single Shard won the prestigious Newbery Medal. In announcing the book's selection as the 2002 winner, the head of the award selection committee explained, "The story shines with dignity and strong values. Park's writing is powerful and precise as she explores universal themes about loyalty and art."

During a 2005 trip to South Korea, first lady Laura Bush reads from Park's book Yum! Yuck! *The picture book for children ages four through eight explores the different sounds that people make in various parts of the world to express surprise, dismay, joy, and other emotions.*

Linda Sue Park and actor Colin Farrell each hold a copy of Click, *the book she coauthored for an Amnesty International fundraiser.*

NEW IDEAS

After winning the Newbery Medal, Park found herself in great demand to give speeches and book reading presentations. In between, she continued to write, producing picture books for younger readers, as well as books for young adults. Most of these titles were set in Korea of many centuries ago.

But Park also wrote about contemporary Korean history, retelling her parents' experiences of living in Korea during the Japanese occupation. *When My Name Was Keoko*, published in 2002, is the story of a Korean sister and brother who, like other Korean people, were forced to take Japanese names during the occupation. Park has explained in interviews that her parents had been forced to change their names. Her mother became Keoko and her father, Nabu—both are names Park uses in her book.

Not all of Park's work is based on Korea or Korean history. In 2007 the author was one of ten different writers who contributed to making a shared novel. The resulting book, *Click*, was sold as a fundraiser for the human rights organization Amnesty International.

CHAPTER FOUR

Margaret Cho: Stand-up Comic

Through her comedy tours, off-Broadway shows, television appearances, albums and memoirs, comedian Margaret Cho has shared a very personal side of her life with the world. She makes it possible for people to laugh along with her as she discusses issues such as her relationship with her Korean-born mother and father, her inability to lose weight, and her misadventures in life. Her comic style has been described as bold, blunt, and sometimes raw.

Before Cho emerged as a star, Americans had never seen a television show in which the main character was Korean. That changed in 1994 with the broadcast of her groundbreaking television show *All-American Girl*, which had an all-Asian cast of actors. The program chronicled the adventures of Cho's character, a college student named Margaret Kim.

San Francisco-born comedian Margaret Cho bases some of her stand-up routines on the conflicts she has with her traditional, Korean-born parents.

◀ CROSS-CURRENTS ▶

The television show *All-American Girl* explored culture clashes between a traditional Korean mother and her Americanized daughter. For more information about why these conflicts happen, turn to page 52.

Although *All-American Girl* had its share of critics, including Cho herself, it was a first step in bringing Asian characters to television. The fact that no one looked like her in the television programs she had watched while growing up in the 1970s had troubled this child of Korean immigrants.

BECOMING MARGARET

Young Hie Cho and Seung Hoon Cho came to the United States in 1964 from Seoul, South Korea, to attend college. The couple settled in San Francisco, in Haight-Ashbury, a district of the city that became known as the center of the hippie counterculture movement of the 1960s and early 1970s. Their daughter, whom they named Moran Cho, was born in San Francisco on December 5, 1968. A son, Hahn Earl, arrived five years later.

In her early years, Cho hardly saw her father, who because of a problem with his visa was deported a few days after she was born. Seung Hoon Cho eventually was able to return to the United States. When he returned he and his wife established a bookstore in Haight-Ashbury, where Margaret and her brother spent much of their time.

Cho lived in the Haight-Ashbury district of San Francisco during the 1970s and 1980s.

Cho's birth certificate lists her first name as Moran, which her father chose because of its association with a hardy Korean flower that thrives in unsuitable conditions. But while her parents liked the name, their young daughter found it a liability when she got to elementary school: Her classmates teased her by calling her "moron" instead of Moran. When she was 10, she changed her name to the more "American-sounding" Margaret.

FEELING LIKE AN OUTSIDER

Cho has many childhood memories of not fitting in anywhere. In her memoir she explains, "My Koreanness, 'my otherness,' embarrassed me. . . . Since I didn't have friends who I was not related to, and the kids that were cruelest to me were other Koreans, my entire world was an exercise in not belonging."

Margaret attended McAteer High School (now known as San Francisco School of the Arts), a high school that offered various programs in the arts of writing, dance, music, and performance. While there, she joined a high school improvisational group called Batwing Lubricant.

When Cho was 16 years old her improv group made an appearance at a local comedy club. They were a hit, and at that moment Margaret decided what she wanted for her future. She would later write in her memoir:

> I saw, in that dark and smoky club, the rest of my life. I thought if I could just be allowed to go onstage and make people laugh every night that I wouldn't care if I made money or became famous. Just the ability to do it would be payment enough.

Cho was not interested in high school and barely managed to graduate from McAteer in 1988. She disappointed her parents when she told them that she wanted to be a stand-up comic. To reach that goal, she worked an assortment of part-time jobs in San Francisco, and performed when she could at comedy clubs, mostly near college campuses.

ALL-AMERICAN GIRL

After moving to Los Angeles, the aspiring comic caught a big break in 1994 when she won the American Comedy Award for best female stand-up comedienne. Cho's recognition by her peers led ABC network to approach her about doing a TV sitcom, *All-American Girl*.

But problems with the show soon arose. The program's producers criticized Cho's appearance and her ethnic-centered comedy. The pressure to lose weight quickly or risk losing her show led Cho to make some unhealthy decisions. She lost so much weight over a short period of time—around 30 pounds in two weeks—that she needed to be hospitalized with kidney failure.

After only one season, *All-American Girl* was cancelled in March 1995. To deal with disappointment and her negative feelings about herself, Margaret began abusing drugs and alcohol. She would later describe the time as her "four-year depression."

THE COMEBACK

Cho did not talk about the cancellation for several years, but sobriety and distance from it finally allowed her to talk about her personal and professional problems in her new act. In 1999

Actors James Kyson Lee (left) and B. D. Wong (right) pose with Cho at the 25th anniversary gala of the Asian American Arts Alliance, held in 2007 in New York City.

I'm the One That I Want became a one-woman, award-winning off-Broadway show and national tour. The risqué stand-up routine was made into a critically acclaimed concert film and best-selling book of the same name.

That show led to other national tours and concert films. Much of the material continued to consist of rants against racism, complaints about conflicts with her parents, and questions over her identity as a Korean American. Tirades about politics and the call for society to guarantee equal rights for people regardless of gender, sexual orientation, or appearance are also a part of her comedy routines. In 2005 the edgy comedian published a collection of essays reflecting her political activism in a book called *I Have Chosen to Stay and Fight*.

NEW DIRECTIONS

In May 2007 Margaret Cho was recognized by the Asian-American community for her work in entertainment. That month she performed at the Asian Excellence Awards, where she was honored with an Outstanding Comedian award.

Cho has returned to television in *The Cho Show,* on the cable television network VH1. The reality sitcom, which first broadcast in August 2008, follows Margaret, her parents, and other people in her life who inspire her comedy as it features actual events in Cho's life. She serves as executive producer, maintaining her comedic style of "anything goes" in her program.

Cho has also been tapped to appear in an hour-long series called *Drop Dead Diva*, starring Broadway actress Brooke Elliott, scheduled to broadcast on Lifetime in the summer of 2009. Cho lives in Los Angeles with her husband, a performance artist and writer, Al Ridenour.

CHAPTER FIVE

Hines Ward, Jr.: Super Bowl MVP

Pittsburgh Steelers Hines Ward, Jr., has set many National Football League (NFL) records as a wide receiver and is one of the top pro football players in the United States. Ward, who is biracial, is the first Korean American to win the coveted Super Bowl Most Valuable Player (MVP) award.

A DIFFICULT START

Hines Ward, Jr., was born on March 8, 1976, in Seoul, South Korea. He was named after his father, Hines Ward Sr., who was an African-American soldier. Hines's mother, Kim Young Hee, is South Korean. Korean society has traditionally been extremely prejudiced against biracial or mixed-race children and their families. Kim Young Hee's parents quickly disowned their daughter.

Hines lived in Korea for a only a short time. When he was a toddler, his family moved to Atlanta, Georgia. A year later his parents split up, and the courts gave Hines's father custody of the boy because Kim Young Hee did not speak English and could not support him. Hines went to live with his father and paternal grandmother in Monroe, Louisiana.

For the next few years Hines had little contact with his mother, but Kim Young Hee worked hard to get her son back. She learned English and worked three jobs so she had enough money to take care of him.

In 1983 Hines's mother regained custody of her son, and she moved with the boy to Forest Park, a suburb of Atlanta. When he lived in Louisiana, Hines had seen his mother only occasionally, during holidays. At age seven he had to get used to living with a woman he barely knew. Meanwhile, his father, who had remarried, disappeared from his life.

LOST BETWEEN TWO CULTURES

Hines had difficulties adjusting to living again with his mother. For many years he was embarrassed by her and resentful of his playmates, who teased him about having a mother who was

Pittsburgh Steelers wide receiver Hines Ward is the son of an African-American father and a Korean mother.

Hines Ward, Jr.: Super Bowl MVP

Asian and a father who was black. In an interview with *Sports Illustrated*, he explained:

> I was lost. I didn't really know who I was. I didn't have guidance. I was so angry with my father for not being there when I needed him the most. And I was so ashamed of my mother—and for not understanding my culture.

Sports provided an outlet. From a young age Hines proved to be good at whatever sport he played. In eighth grade he was named best athlete. The following year, at Forest Park High School, the freshman was good enough to be on the varsity football team. During his junior and senior years he would start—and star—as quarterback. Hines would later tell an interviewer that excelling at sports gave him the respect that he felt he lacked in other areas of his life. "If you were the best player, people were going to love you regardless," he said. "People didn't look at race. I loved getting voted best athlete in school because as the best athlete there was less teasing."

Because Ward was a standout on his high school football team, college recruiters soon came calling with offers of football scholarships. As a recent immigrant, Ward's mother had no idea what they were talking about. When she understood that a football scholarship would allow her son to attend college for free, she agreed to let him play.

In 1994 Ward enrolled at the University of Georgia, in Athens, where he played for the Bulldogs as a wide receiver, as well as tailback and quarterback. He set many records and earned All-Southeastern Conference honors on the field for the Bulldogs while earning a degree in economics.

STEELERS STAR

After finishing college, Hines Ward was picked in the third round of the 1998 NFL draft by the Pittsburgh Steelers. Not being chosen in an earlier round made him work harder to

prove his worth to his team as a wide receiver—and to himself. He also worked hard to become a starter—which did not occur until his second season with the Steelers.

Through the years Ward has been a valuable asset for the Steelers. The highlights of his career include breaking Pittsburgh Steelers records for receptions, receiving touchdowns and receiving yardage, being selected multiple times as Steelers MVP, and being named Super Bowl MVP in 2006. In addition to being the first Korean-American athlete to achieve that honor, he is also only one of five wide receivers in the history of the Super Bowl to earn the MVP award.

After gaining fame in 2006 as an NFL Super Bowl Most Valuable Player, Ward traveled with his mother, Kim Young Hee (right) to South Korea, where he was welcomed as a hero by the Korean media.

HELPING BIRACIAL KIDS

In April 2006 Ward and his mother flew to South Korea for a long-planned 10-day visit to her homeland. In Korea, he received a great deal of publicity. Korean reporters, thrilled by the visit from the first Korean-American Super Bowl MVP, followed Hines and his mother as they visited various landmarks.

Ward told interviewers that he appreciated being in Korea and having the opportunity to learn more about his birthplace. He also said he was pleased at the welcome they received, especially since his mother had previously been shunned because he was biracial. He told *Sports Illustrated*:

In April 2006 Ward met with children of mixed racial origins in Seoul, South Korea.

> This completes me. I never really got into my Korean heritage, as far as what being Korean means. It seems like I've been living with it the whole time, and I've never really gotten in touch with it . . . There are some things my mom has hidden from me, like I never met my grandmother [because] my mom was disowned by her family.

There was so much animosity toward her because she had an African American child. It's like it took me winning the Super Bowl MVP to be accepted.

The Super Bowl MVP winner decided to use his celebrity status in Korea to help biracial and mixed-race kids, especially those dealing with discrimination. While in Korea, Ward met with representatives of Pearl S. Buck International (PSBI), a charitable organization that provides adoption, sponsorship, and educational services to children around the world. PSBI arranged several meetings between Ward and disadvantaged Korean children for what he called "hope-sharing."

In May 2006 Ward returned to South Korea to announce the creation of the Hines Ward Helping Hands Founda-

◀ **CROSS-CURRENTS** ▶

To learn more about how the Hines Ward Helping Hands Foundation inspires biracial kids, turn to page 53.

tion, a charity organization to help combat the discrimination faced by biracial children in Korea. At that time, he also announced he was donating $1 million of his own money to the foundation. Ward has said that he relates to the situation of biracial kids, having been one himself. Helping the kids is important to him, he says: "I have always wondered what my purpose was here on Earth. It wasn't just to play football. It was to do bigger things."

The Hines Ward Helping Hands Foundation also helps kids from single-family homes throughout western Pennsylvania. It focuses on promoting literacy and providing services to disadvantaged children in the region. Hines is a father himself of a son, Jaden, born in March 2004, to his wife, Simone.

CHAPTER SIX

The Ahn Trio: Musical Sister Act

The three Ahn sisters have played on MTV and at concert halls around the world, drawing attention for their unusual combination of classical and modern music, as well as for their stylish appearance. Known as the Ahn Trio, twin sisters Maria and Lucia, and younger sister Angella, are famous for making classical music accessible and exciting to younger audiences. Their crossover music covers an assortment of genres, including rock, jazz, and hip-hop.

While the technical virtuosity of these three musicians is beyond question, they have met resistance from some in the classical music world for trying to introduce new sounds. Angella responds, "We play contemporary music to reflect the world we live in, reflecting all the different sounds of today. And we hope to bring classical music to fans of all musical genres."

Korean-born sisters (from left to right) Angella, Lucia, and Maria Ahn received classical training but perform music of various genres in their concerts.

SEOUL SISTERS

Maria and Lucia, who is ten minutes younger than her twin, were born on August 30, 1970, in Seoul, South Korea. Angella came along two years later, on June 10, 1972. Their mother, Young Joon Rhee, worked as a journalist and their father, Kwang-Yong Ahn, as a book publisher. Although the parents did not play musical instruments themselves, they were huge fans of classical music. The girls grew up listening to classical music on records and attending live performances as soon as they were old enough to sit still through them.

The road to what would become the Ahn Trio began for Lucia when she was in kindergarten and became enthralled by the piano in her classroom. The five-year-old begged her mother to let her take lessons. It was not until a year later that Young Joon Rhee finally relented, and Lucia began studying with a piano teacher.

Not wanting to be left out, Angella and Maria also asked to take music lessons. They both started with piano but soon moved on to other instruments: Maria took up the cello and Angella learned to play the violin. The girls were child prodigies. They first played together publicly in 1979, when they were featured on Korean television.

AHN TRIO

In 1981 the girls' parents split up and Young Joon Rhee moved with the children to the United States. The family settled in New Jersey, and the girls went to the pre-college music program at Julliard, the prestigious school of music in New York City.

The musicians focused on playing chamber music, a form of classical music featuring a small number of

The Ahn Trio is a classical piano trio, with Angella playing violin, Lucia on piano, and Maria playing cello. Piano trio music, which originated in the 18th century, traditionally includes works by classical composers such as Joseph Haydn, Wolfgang Amadeus Mozart, and Ludwig van Beethoven.

The Ahn Trio: Musical Sister Act

instruments—in their case, the piano, violin, and cello. (The name *chamber music* comes from the fact that the instruments can fit into and be played in a small room, or chamber.) In 1992 the Ahn Trio won raves from critics and top honors at the Alliance Northeast Competition for Chamber Ensembles. That same year they won first prize at the Coleman Chamber Ensemble Competition.

FINDING FAME

The Ahn Trio was giving regular concert performances in 1995, when it released its debut album, *Paris Rio,* to critical acclaim. The classical CD contained compositions by Maurice Ravel and Heitor Villa-Lobos. It was followed in 1999 by *Dvořák, Suk, Shostakovich: Piano Trios,* which featured the classical composers Antonín Dvořák, Dmitry Shostakovich, and Josef Suk. The album won an ECHO, Germany's version of a Grammy Award.

In 1997 the Ahn Trio appeared on the television program *MTV Unplugged,* where the three musicians supported rock singer Bryan Adams playing some of his hits. The experience inspired them to move away from only classical compositions in their third album. In *Ahn-Plugged,* they play some commissioned pieces by contemporary composers such as Kenji Bunch and Eric Ewazen—who were also alumni of Juilliard.

The group continued to explore the work of contemporary classical and popular music composers in a fourth album, *Groovebox,* released in 2002. That CD opened with a rock classic by the Doors, "Riders on the Storm."

Their talent, good looks, and fashion sense ensured that the Ahns were noticed by the media. Lucia, Angella, and Maria were featured in news stories and in fashion and entertainment magazines such as *Vogue* and *GQ.* The three also modeled in advertisements for the clothing retailer Gap Stores and for fashion designer Anne Klein. *People* magazine listed the sisters as among the "50 Most Beautiful People" of 2003.

CONCERT LIFE

For many years the Ahn Trio kept a busy tour schedule—performing at more than 100 events per year. But in 2007 the musicians told interviewers that they wanted more time for their lives and were no longer going to perform as often.

The Ahn Trio attracts a wide audience to its concerts, as the piano trio shares classical and other music genres with a new generation. Many performances take place at colleges, where the sisters discuss their music with their audiences and give workshops and classes to students. As part of the Lincoln Center Institute Program, they also hold public school clinics in cities where they perform.

Some of the Ahn Trio performances have been concert benefits—fundraisers for agencies and organizations that support Koreans living in the United States. Organizations supported by the Ahn Trio include the Korean American Community Services, in

The Lincoln Center for the Performing Arts, in New York City. The Ahn Trio has frequently performed at the Center's indoor venue, Alice Tully Hall, and at its outdoor venue, in Damrosch Park.

The Ahn Trio: Musical Sister Act

◀ CROSS-CURRENTS ▶

To learn more about some of the Korean community service organizations that have benefited from Ahn Trio concert performance fundraisers, turn to page 54.

Chicago; The K. W. Lee Center for Leadership, in Los Angeles; and the Korean Community Services of Metropolitan New York. Angella, Lucia, and Maria have also performed at concerts to raise money for children's relief programs in North Korea and for Asians for Miracle Marrow Matches, an organization that matches bone marrow donors with cancer patients who need life-saving transplants.

A NEW SOUND

A newspaper music reviewer once described the Ahn Trio and the appeal of the group's sound:

> With their multicultural assortment of composers and huge talent, these women have a modernist, fusion sensibility that is perfect for our age. Their take on chamber music is intimate, yet grand, innovative, yet classic. To the listener, it's a revolution.

In May 2008, the three musicians were directly involved with the production of their fifth album, produced under the L.A.M.P. label, which stands for Lucia Angella Maria Productions. *Lullaby for My Favorite Insomniac* contains music written especially for the group, as well as established compositions. The tracks feature classical sounds, as well as rock, jazz, and hip-hop. On the Ahn Trio's Web site, Maria Ahn described what she and her sister were trying to do in the *Favorite Insomniac* album:

> [W]e've tried to create a new wave of music . . . a fusion of our very traditionally acoustic instruments with the best parts of the various genres of "pop" music existing today (rock, indie, electronica, r&b, alternative), thereby creating a sound that is distinctively our own.

SuChin Pak: Television News Correspondent

As an MTV correspondent, SuChin Pak has interviewed celebrities, covered shows like the *MTV Movie Awards* and *MTV Video Music Awards*, and co-hosted MTV's Grammy pre-shows. The first Asian American to represent MTV, Pak got her start on television in the mid-1990s, at a time when there were not many Asian-American women on television.

STRADDLING TWO CULTURES

SuChin Pak was born on August 15, 1976, in Seoul, South Korea. When she was five years old her parents, Sung and Chong Pak, moved to a suburb outside San Francisco, California.

SuChin Pak became a familiar face on the cable television network MTV after being hired in 2001 as a news correspondent.

SuChin's mother and father came to the United States because they wanted better economic and educational opportunities. Neither of them learned to speak English very well. But they made it clear to their daughter from an early age that they valued education. They expected her to be a lawyer or have some kind of professional career when she grew up.

SuChin's parents were very traditional. They spoke only Korean inside the home and English outside. In an interview, SuChin recalled her childhood: "Growing up inside my house, it was like Korea circa 1968. Outside my house, it was America in 1985, so I've always lived in a kind of dichotomy of American identity."

BREAKING INTO TV

The Paks did not even own a television set when SuChin got her first television job at age 16—without even looking for it. At the time she was a student at James Logan High School, in Union City. She was participating in an after-school activity called Youth for Government when a local television station, KGO-TV, interviewed her. The short clip was seen by the station's program director, who offered SuChin a job hosting a San Francisco Bay Area television show called *Straight Talkin' Teens*. One of her first interviews was with rapper Ice T, whom the nervous Pak accidentally referred to on-air as Ice Pick. Both she and Ice T took her mistake in stride.

SuChin's parents had problems at first with the idea of their daughter appearing on television: "They were very very not happy about my getting the local TV show," SuChin later told an interviewer. That kind of behavior went against tradition, she explained: "Girls are girls and quiet. Don't speak unless spoken to. I was voted 'most shy' in seventh grade! Can you even believe it?"

After graduating from high school, Pak enrolled at the University of California at Berkeley. While there, Pak sent off an audition tape to the headquarters of the PBS science-based show *Newton's Apple.* She was offered a job as one of the five hosts of the nationally broadcast program, a position she held from 1996 to 1997. While working as a host for two television shows, SuChin maintained her full-time course load at Berkeley, where she majored in political science.

After graduation, Pak had to make a decision about whether to attend law school, as her parents wished, or continue in television. She explains, "I kept trying not to ask myself the question that I really wanted to ask, which was, do I really want to do this for a living? Of course the answer was yes."

Going against her parents' wishes was difficult for Pak, who is close to her family and even as an adult still feels the need to please them. She would later write about the strong connection she has with her parents:

> It's a lot of pressure, to not only live successfully for yourself, but for your entire family. I think that's why I've always been so driven; I think if I was just doing this for myself, I'm not sure I would have worked so hard at school, at my job. But knowing that what you do helps your family, that your family depends on your success . . . it's a huge pressure, but it can also be a great motivator.

ON MTV

In 2000 Pak left San Francisco for New York City after agreeing to cohost an episode of *Trackers,* a musical/talk show broadcast on the Oxygen Network. But she became even more visible to television audiences the following year, after accepting a job as MTV correspondent for its news division. Pak has said that she believes MTV hired her because "I told the truth in my audition; that I was there because I was really interested in youth culture and what it means to be an American."

Pak interviews Jessica Simpson (left) during the actress/ singer's October 2006 appearance on the MTV show Total Request Live.

As a news correspondent SuChin covered MTV awards programs and reported for *MTV News*. She was part of documentaries such as *Social History of Hair*. And she reported on more serious events, including the aftermath of the terrorist attacks of September 11, 2001, and the tsunami that devastated Southeast Asia in December 2004. As a video jockey on *Total Request Live (TRL)*, she interviewed numerous popular celebrities, including Justin Timberlake, Mariah Carey, Fred Durst, and Britney Spears.

When MTV launched its public service Choose or Lose campaign to encourage young people to vote in the 2004 presidential election, Pak reported on people trying to make a difference through politics. That same year she hosted an MTV series that was close to her heart. *My Life (Translated)* focused on challenges faced by children of new immigrants in the United States. Of her own experience as the child of Korean immigrants, she says, "[M]y whole life I juggled these two identities. How do you fit in in a country that is home, but it is not where you come from?"

BRANCHING OUT

In June 2008 Pak joined with CBS News science and technology correspondent Daniel Sieberg to cohost a daily series called *G Word*, which airs on the eco-lifestyle television network Planet Green. The daily series gives information and ideas on how to make good environmental choices in life, in areas such as the home, fashion and design, food, and shopping.

In 2008 and 2009 Pak also hosted an original series for MTV called *Engine Room*. Created by MTV and Hewlett-Packard, the competition brings together young digital artists from around the world. They solve various technology challenges by creating animations, Web sites, short films, and other projects. The short-form online series airs on the MTV college network mtvU and on MTV channels around the world.

In addition to her many appearances as a television host for MTV shows and Green Planet, Pak has played bit parts in films, too. She appears as herself in the comedies *Deck the Halls* (2006) and *The Rocker* (2008).

In 2008 Pak became a cohost of Planet Green's program G Word.

◀ **CROSS-CURRENTS** ▶

On the MTV My Life (Translated) Web site, SuChin Pak shared many personal thoughts about being both Korean and American. To learn more, turn to page 54.

CHAPTER EIGHT

Michelle Wie: Pro Golfer

Michelle Wie first held a golf club in her hand when she was four years old. Today she is a golf superstar who has set many records. The young woman is known for her fluid swing and powerful 300-foot drives on the golf course. But she is also famous for her determination to compete against men, as well as women, in professional golf events. Her ultimate goal, she has said, is to participate in the Masters Golf Tournament, one of the major championships of men's professional golf.

Despite some injuries and setbacks, the 6-foot Korean-American athlete continues to generate excitement on the links. Her celebrity has resonated with Nike, Omega, Sony, and other companies that have been generous sponsors. *Forbes* reported that between June 2006 and June 2007 Wie earned $19 million in endorsement income. In December 2007 the magazine named her as one of the country's "Top 20 Earners Under 25."

GOLFING PHENOM

Michelle Wie was born in Honolulu, Hawaii, on October 11, 1989. Her father, Byung Wook "B. J." Wie, and mother, Hyung-Kyong "Bo" Wie, met in Hawaii after emigrating from South Korea in the 1980s. Bo had been an amateur golf champion in Korea but worked as a real estate agent in the United States. B. J., who also enjoyed golfing, was a professor at the University of Hawaii.

Because Bo and B. J. loved to spend time golfing, it was natural for them to introduce their only child to the sport at an early age. Michelle was just four years old when she began to learn the game. Her parents also taught her to swim and play tennis, and she took lessons in gymnastics and ballet. But it soon became clear that golf was where her talents lay.

From the very start, B. J. encouraged Michelle to imitate the swing of golf superstar Tiger Woods. To inspire Michelle, B. J. placed posters of Tiger on the young girl's bedroom walls. The media would refer to Tiger when they first noticed Michelle in 2000. It was reported that the 10-year-old, 5 foot 7 inch girl could hit the ball a distance of 260 yards. One newspaper headline that year reported on the young golf phenomenon in a story under the headline "Following in Tiger's Tracks."

Pro golfer Michelle Wie is watched by her father and sometimes caddy, B. J., as she completes her swing during a 2006 tournament.

PLAYING AGAINST THE PROS

At age 11 Michelle became the youngest winner of the Jennie K. Wilson Invitational, an amateur women's tournament in Hawaii. A year later she was playing against professional women golfers— becoming the youngest person to qualify for an event on the Ladies Professional Golf Association (LPGA) tour. In 2003, at

Twelve-year-old Michelle poses with her father, B. J., and mother, Bo.

age 13, Michelle won the U.S. Women's Amateur Public Links Championship, becoming the event's youngest winner.

In January 2004, 14-year-old Wie was almost 6 feet tall when she became the youngest person to play in a Professional Golfers' Association (PGA) Tour event, the Sony Open in Hawaii. Few females make the cut that allows them to compete in PGA Tour events. Michelle shot a 68, setting the record for the lowest score by a woman competing against men. She missed making the cut by just one shot, but at the same time she beat 62 of the best professional men's golfers.

In June 2005 Michelle was still an amateur when she took second place at the McDonald's LPGA Championship, which normally allowed only professional women golfers. She finished three shots behind Annika Sorenstam, who was 19 years older. That October, shortly before reaching her 16th birthday, Michelle turned pro. During the rest of 2005 and in 2006, she finished in the top five in the 16 events she competed in.

UPS AND DOWNS

Wie attended Panahou School, a college preparatory school in Honolulu. She was a gifted student who achieved high grades in math, English, and science. In April 2006, when she was a junior, she became the only 16-year-old to crack *Time*'s "Top 100 People Who Shape Our World." The magazine recognized Michelle for her number two ranking (at the time) in women's golf, her tremendous endorsement income, and her refusal to be limited to ladies-only golf. The magazine described Wie's intention to be first woman to play in the Masters as "driving her way straight through golf's formidable gender barriers."

The following year, however, was a rough one. It started out badly as Michelle attended the Sony Open in January with a hurt right wrist. In February she suffered a broken left wrist and tendonitis (an inflammation of the hand), injuries that resulted

An exhilarated Wie pumps her fist after finishing in the top 20 of the qualifying tournament at the LPGA International held in Daytona Beach, Florida. The accomplishment earned her the right to play in all 2009 LPGA competitions.

in her completing only three tournaments in 2007. The loss of strength in her hands and wrists reduced her ability to perform well on the links and she finished far down in the field in all three events.

When asked that September about the struggles of Michelle Wie, Tiger Woods was optimistic about her chances of winning pro tournaments. He said, "I have a feeling that once she does win and the floodgates open, she'll win a bunch of events. Once you break that hurdle, I think she'll learn from it and obviously win a lot more."

LPGA Commissioner Carolyn Bivens agreed, stating, "It was unrealistic to expect any player, at any age, to enter the LPGA and dominate right away. . . . It's way too early to give up on her, and it's way too early to know what kind of career she will have."

GETTING BACK ON TRACK

Some critics attribute Michelle Wie's difficulties to the fact that she went pro at an early age, especially when compared to other professional golfers. (Tiger Woods went pro when he was 21.) But she has said that she has no regrets about the past. She told an interviewer:

> I don't regret any choices I made when I was younger. You only have one try at life, and whether it's a good decision or a bad decision, it is a decision, and what are you gonna do? There's nothing I can do about it. I just learn to accept things in life. Things happen, and you've just got to move forward.

After graduating from high school in 2007, Wie was accepted by Stanford University, in Palo Alto, California. She took some time off from pro golf to attend classes but then reduced her university schedule so she could began playing again.

In late 2008 Wie secured her LPGA Tour card for 2009—the card guarantees a golfer the right to play in LPGA tournaments (previously Michelle entered tournaments on sponsor's exemptions or by special invitation). To earn the right to play in LPGA tournaments, golfers must end up in the top 20 in qualifying tournaments, also known as LPGA Q-School. Wie played conservatively during the December 2008 tournaments, and made the cut.

Her coach, David Leadbetter noted at the time that Wie was enjoying her game again. He added, "She doesn't have to live up to other people's expectations, now. She simply has to live up to her own."

◀ **CROSS-CURRENTS** ▶

There are many other talented pro golfers besides Michelle Wie who are of Korean-American heritage. To learn more, turn to page 55.

ATTITUDES TOWARD IMMIGRATION

The Gallup Organization surveys people around the world to determine public opinion regarding various political, social, and economic issues. One issue that Gallup has researched over the years is immigration to the United States. In general, Americans have a positive view of immigration, reports the Gallup Web site:

> Three in four [Americans] have consistently said it has been good for the United States in the past, and a majority says it is good for the nation today. However, Americans still seem interested in limiting the amount of immigration.

When asked in a July 2008 Gallup survey about the level of immigration into the United States, 39 percent of Americans favored decreasing the number of immigrants allowed into the country, a decrease from 45 percent a year earlier. However, only 18 percent believe it should be increased.

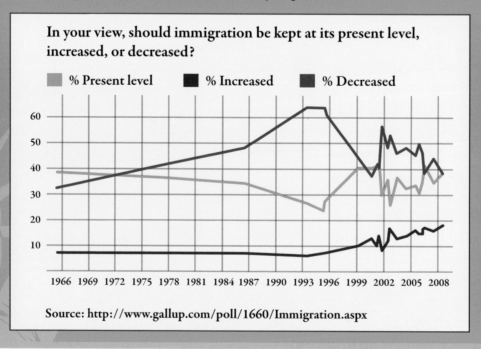

In your view, should immigration be kept at its present level, increased, or decreased?

■ % Present level   ■ % Increased   ■ % Decreased

Source: http://www.gallup.com/poll/1660/Immigration.aspx

PARTNERS IN HEALTH

More than 20 years ago, before they had even graduated from Harvard Medical School, Jim Yong Kim and his friend, Paul Farmer, started a nonprofit group in Boston called Partners in Health (PIH). Starting with a single clinic providing free medical care in Haiti, the charity has evolved into a global public health network that provides health care, food, water, and education to the poor. Today, the countries served by Partners in Health include Haiti, Peru, Russia, Mexico, Guatemala, Rwanda, and the United States.

PIH partners with people in the community, creating a support system to ensure that patients who need daily treatments do not get sick again. Partners in Health does this by training and employing laypeople to look after neighbors, encouraging them to get medical treatment and ensuring that those with diseases such as AIDS or TB take medications on schedule. PIH also helps ensure a community's food supply by providing training in farming methods and offering small loans to farmers or to groups trying to establish small businesses.

The charity's multiple-pronged approach to treating people with AIDS and other infectious diseases has been embraced by the World Health Organization for use in developing countries. PIH has also partnered with the Bill and Melinda Gates Foundation and the William J. Clinton Presidential Foundation.

The story of Partners in Health is told in a 2003 biography about Paul Farmer (left) entitled Mountains Beyond Mountains.

ENGLISH AS A SECOND LANGUAGE

Before she made her living as a writer, Linda Sue Park taught English as a second language to adults at Brooklyn College, in New York City, and at the English Language Center of Rochester Institute of Technology. ESL programs typically include instruction in listening comprehension, speaking, reading, writing, and grammar. These intensive-learning classes can be difficult for adult students who are trying to learn English while managing jobs and families.

One of Linda Sue's books, *Mung-Mung: A Foldout Book of Animal Sounds*, was based on a get-to-know-you exercise she used with new ESL students. It involved discussing the different words used in various languages to describe sounds animals make. For example, Park would ask each student to answer a question like, "What does a dog say in your country?" (*Mung-mung* is Korean for "woof woof.") The ESL exercise evolved into a picture book published in 2004.

As the United States becomes more culturally diverse, ESL programs have helped non-English speaking immigrants learn the fundamentals of English so they can deal with day-to-day life and not rely on others to translate. According to a 2007 Gallup poll, a large majority of Americans believe that immigrants should become competent in English. The poll reported that 77 percent of respondents believed that becoming proficient in English should be a condition for immigrants to remain in the United States.

CULTURE CLASHES

Based on the stand-up comedy routines of Cho, the ABC television series *All-American Girl* looked at the culture clashes between a traditional Korean mother and her Americanized daughter. In one episode of the show, for example, Cho's character dated a non-Korean boy, and her mother voiced strong disapproval because her daughter was dating outside their ethnic group.

Like Cho, other first- and second-generation immigrant children may find themselves disagreeing with their parents over who is considered acceptable to date. Other issues may include the importance of excelling in school and music or choices in clothing or a future career. It can be difficult for children of immigrants growing up in the United States when the traditional ways of a parent's homeland clash with American values.

Korean-American counselor Josephine Kim of the Harvard Graduate School of Education has studied mental health issues among Asian Americans. She attributes intergenerational conflicts—clashes between immigrant parents and their kids—to situations in which Korean parents work extensive hours outside the home. In trying to make money to make a better life for their families, they are absent from and uninvolved with the lives of their kids.

Biracial children living in Korea face extreme discrimination in education, employment, and marriage because society traditionally emphasizes that its people have only Korean heritage. When Hines Ward traveled to South Korea, he wanted to meet with biracial children to show them it was possible to endure prejudice and other challenges and come out on top.

In establishing the Hines Ward Helping Hands Foundation, Ward partnered with Pearl S. Buck International Korea, which also strives to help biracial and mixed-race children in Korea. Each year the staff of Pearl S. Buck International pick a group of these children to travel to the United States, based on a short essay written about their hopes and dreams for the future. Ward's foundation pays for the trip.

The Korean children spend time with Ward during their visit—he has typically met their plane at the airport—and they attend a Pittsburgh Steelers football game, where they get to see him play. Ward has said, "It's a great feeling to bring these kids all the way from Seoul . . . and really give them the chance to not give up on their hopes and dreams, and see how different America is—that they can have a positive future in their lives."

South Korean prime minister Han Myung-sook (right) shakes hands with Hines Ward after their meeting on May 29, 2006, in Seoul. That day he announced the establishment of his foundation to help mixed-race children in South Korea.

KOREAN COMMUNITY SERVICE ORGANIZATIONS

When immigrants come to the United States, they typically seek the help of people from their native land who are already living in the country. Through them, the new immigrants can find a commonality of experience, heritage, and comfort. This arrangement can be as simple as one family helping out another one. However, often help is provided by a more formal system that has developed to meet a perceived gap in social services.

In areas of the country where there are substantial numbers of Korean immigrants, organizations have emerged to serve local needs. The Ahn Trio has given concerts to benefit some of these organizations:

Korean American Community Services (KACS): Based in Chicago, this organization provides services such as child care, housing for senior citizens, health programs, English language and other educational instruction, and employment counseling.

K. W. Lee Center for Leadership: Based in the Koreatown area of Los Angeles, the Center provides educational programs and training to help youth in the area develop leadership skills.

Korean Community Services of Metropolitan New York (KCS): This agency assists low-income Korean families and recent Korean immigrants, as well as other members of the community. Some KCS programs, which help groups such as the elderly, new immigrants, and parents, include job training, English language education, public health care, and child care.

BEING A BICULTURAL TEEN

Through her MTV series *My Life (Translated)*, SuChin Pak told the stories of teens struggling with the same issues she faced while growing up. Like other immigrant groups, young Korean Americans can feel torn between identifying with parents and finding their own path in the world. In trying to bridge the gap between what it means to be Korean and American, SuChin Pak has said she seeks to be a super American who picks and chooses between the bits and pieces of both worlds to come up with an effective hybrid version of the two. She explains:

I love being Korean. I love that my mother gets up at 5 in the morning to cook me a warm breakfast before I get on a plane. I love that my parents only know how to use the cell phone to call me or my brother. I love that I would never disrespect my parents, even if it means that I've sacrificed some parts of my life. But I also love that I can talk freely about these things because I live in a culture that encourages expression. . . . I love that I can work at a place that respects my opinions and values my point of view. I love that I can appreciate the fine art of Justin Timberlake and still cook a mean KalBi dish at home.

OTHER KOREAN-AMERICAN GOLFERS

Anthony Kim (1985–): Born in Los Angeles, California, Kim was part of winning USA team in the 2005 Walker Cup and 2008 Ryder Cup. After turning pro in 2006, he finished in the top 100 of the official world golf rankings in his rookie season. He won his first PGA Tour tournament in May 2008.

Christina Kim (1984–): Born in San Jose, California, Kim is known for her flamboyant dress but also for earning LPGA Rookie of the Year in 2003. In 2004 she became the youngest player to reach $1 million in earnings, although that record was broken the following year.

Kevin Na (1983–): Born in Seoul, South Korea, Na came to the United States when he was eight. In 2001 he turned pro and subsequently found success playing on the PGA Tour. He won the 2006 Mark Christopher Charity Classic and the 2002 Volvo Masters of Asia. At age 18, he became an American citizen.

Angela Park (1988–): Born in Brazil to parents of South Korean heritage, Park came to the United States when she was nine years old. She turned pro in April 2006 and the following year was named the LPGA Rookie of the Year. A naturalized citizen as of 2008, Park also holds Brazilian citizenship.

NOTES

CHAPTER 1

p. 11: "I love America because . . ." Quoted in Timothy Cox, "Korean-Americans Find Good Life in City," *Augusta Chronicle*, June 1, 2008.

CHAPTER 2

p. 13: "[The lectures] made me . . ." Quoted in Stephen Byrd, "World Leader in Medicine Chalks Up His Values to Muscatine Upbringing," *Muscatine Journal*, November 26, 2005. http://www.muscatinejournal.com/articles/2005/11/26/news/doc438902cfa46df387810751.prt

p. 15: "It's a huge . . ." Quoted in Ken Gewert, *Harvard University Gazette*, October 9, 2003. www.hno.harvard.edu/gazette/2003/10.09/01-macarthurs.html

p. 17: "[O]nly a handful of . . ." Jim Yong Kim, *Harvard International Review*, Summer 2007, vol. 29, issue 2, 20.

CHAPTER 3

p. 19: "I was a huge reader . . ." Quoted in Clifford Thompson, editor, *Current Biography Yearbook 2002*, 447.

p. 20: "I have been writing . . ." Quoted in Lisa Kumar, editor, *Something About the Author*, vol. 173, Detroit, Mich.: Thomson Gale, 139–140.

p. 21: "The story shines with . . ." Quoted in "Park, Wiesner Win Newbery, Caldecott Medals," American Library Association [Press release],

January 21, 2002. http://www.ala.org/Template.cfm?Section=archive&template=/contentmanagement/contentdisplay.cfm&ContentID=14059

CHAPTER 4

p. 25: "My Koreanness, 'my otherness' . . ." Margaret Cho, *I'm The One That I Want*, New York: Ballantine Books, 2001, 15.

p. 25: "I saw, in that dark and smoky club . . ." Cho, *I'm the One That I Want*, 70.

p. 26: "four-year depression." Jennifer Tung, "Television Nearly Destroyed Me," *New York Post*, June 14, 1999.

CHAPTER 5

p. 30: "I was lost. . . ." Quoted in Karl Taro Greenfield, "The Long Way Home," *Sports Illustrated*, May 15, 2008, 60.

p. 30: "If you were the best . . ." Quoted in Greenfield, "The Long Way Home," *Sports Illustrated*.

p. 32: "This completes me. I never . . ." Quoted in Greenfield, "The Long Way Home," *Sports Illustrated*.

p. 33: "I have always wondered . . ." Rob Rossi, "Hines Ward Shows a Lot of Heart Off the Field, Too," *Pittsburgh Tribune*, December 17, 2006.

CHAPTER 6

p. 34: "We play contemporary music to . . ." Quoted in Delma J. Francis, "Rock Ahn, Sisters,"

Star Tribune (Minneapolis, Minnesota), March 2, 2007.

p. 38: "With their multicultural assortment . . ." Diane Wright, *Seattle Times*, February 6, 2007.

p. 38: "[W]e've tried to create . . ." Maria Ahn, "Upcoming New CD Release of 'Lullaby for My Favorite Insomniac' on SonyBMG,"Bio, Ahn Trio. http://www.ahntrio.com/v2/

CHAPTER 7

p. 40: "Growing up inside my house . . ." Quoted in Jeff Weiner, "SuChin Pak Talks Race, Politics and Role of Youth at Symposium," *Central Florida Future*, April 2, 2008.

p. 40: "They were very very . . ." N. F. Mendoza, "The Energizer Host and Traveler: Suchin Pak Packs a Lot into a Day," *Los Angeles Times*, October 15, 1995.

p. 41: "I kept trying not to ask myself . . ." Quoted in Mallory Reed, "SuChin Pak Speaks in Voices of Color Series," *The Spectator,* March 3, 2008.

p. 41: "It's a lot of pressure, to not only live . . ." SuChin Pak, "SuChin's Journal," MTV My Life (Translated), November 18, 2004. http://www.mtv.com/bands/m/mylifetranslated/index2.jhtml

p. 41: "I told the truth in my audition . . ." Quoted in Reed, "SuChin Pak Speaks in Voices of Color Series," *The Spectator.*

p. 43: "[M]y whole life I juggled . . ." Quoted in Reed, "SuChin Pak Speaks in Voices of Color Series," *The Spectator.*

CHAPTER 8

p. 47: "driving her way . . ." Jeff Chu, "Michelle Wie," *Time*, April 30, 2006. http://www.time.com/time/magazine/article/0,9171,1187323,00.html

p. 48: "I have a feeling that once . . ." Quoted in Steve DiMeglio, "Falling Star, or Speed Bump? Wie's Career Took Wrong Turn in '07," *USA Today*, October 16, 2007, C3.

p. 48: "It was unrealistic to expect . . ." Quoted in DeMeglio, "Falling Star, Or Speed Bump? Wie's Career Took Wrong Turn in '07."

p. 49: "I don't regret any choices . . ." Quoted in Melinda Waldrop, "Wie Has No Regrets: She's Yet To Find Her Professional Path, But Michelle Wie Isn't Questioning Her Previous Career Decisions," *Daily Press*, May 7, 2008.

p. 49: "She doesn't have to . . ." Quoted in John Garrity, "Michelle Wie Is Finally a Member of the LPGA Tour," *Sports Illustrated*, December 8, 2008.

CROSS-CURRENTS

p. 50: "Three in four [Americans] have . . ." "Immigration," Gallup, 2008. http://www.gallup.com/poll/1660/Immigration.aspx

p. 53: "It's a great feeling to bring . . ." Quoted in David M. Brown, "Ward Thankful to Give Back to South Korean Kids," *Pittsburgh Tribune-Review*, December 15, 2007.

p. 54: "I love being Korean . . ." SuChin Pak, "SuChin's Journal," MTV My Life (Translated)," April 2, 2004. http://www.mtv.com/bands/m/mylifetranslated/index4.jhtml

GLOSSARY

Amerasian—of American and Asian ancestry.

cold war—a period of tension and hostility from 1945 to 1991 between the governments of the United States and Soviet Union due to differences in economic and political policies.

communist—describing a form of government in which all property and businesses are publicly owned and controlled by the state.

emigrate—to move away from a country to settle in another country or region.

ensemble—a small group of musicians, actors, or dancers who perform together.

genre—a type, class, or category of music or literature based on similarity of style or form.

Grammy—an annual music award given by the National Academy of Recording Arts and Sciences for outstanding achievement in the recording industry.

immigrate—to move to a new country or region.

medical anthropology—the study of the relationships between socio-cultural factors and the control of disease and maintenance of health.

naturalized citizen—a person who has officially acquired the rights of nationality in a country after being born somewhere else.

Newbery Medal—named for the 18th century bookseller John Newbery, the award given by the American Library Association to the most distinguished children's book of the year.

NFL draft—an annual event conducted by the National Football League in which NFL teams select talented college football players.

poll—a survey, often conducted over the phone, in person, or over the Internet, in which the public's attitudes about specific issues are documented.

prodigy—a young child who displays exceptional talents and abilities.

quota—in immigration law, a fixed maximum number of people allowed to enter a country.

sitcom—short for situation comedy; usually a 30-minute show aired weekly on television featuring the same characters.

United Nations—an international organization established in October 1945 by representatives of 50 countries to promote peace and international cooperation.

visa—government permission to enter a country; the mark or stamp on a passport that allows a foreigner to visit a country for a specific period of time and often for a specific purpose.

wide receiver—offensive player on a football team whose job is to catch passes.

FURTHER READING

Cho, Margaret. *I'm The One That I Want*. New York: Ballantine Books, 2001.

Cummings, Bruce. *Korea's Place in the Sun: A Modern History*. New York: W. W. Norton, 2005.

Kidder, Tracy. *Mountains Beyond Mountains: The Quest of Dr. Paul Farmer, A Man Who Would Cure the World*. New York: Random House, 2003.

Park, Linda Sue. *When My Name Was Keoko*. New York: Clarion Books, 2002.

Sampson, Curt. *Golf Dads: Fathers, Sons, and the Greatest Game*. Boston: Houghton Mifflin Company, 2008.

Sandler, Michael. *Hines Ward and the Pittsburgh Steelers: Super Bowl XL*. New York: Bearport Publishing, 2007.

INTERNET RESOURCES

http://www.ahntrio.com
The Ahn Trio's official Web site features the chamber ensemble's music, video clips, and tour information.

http://www.gallup.com
The Web site of the Gallup Organization, an international polling institute that monitors public opinion, features various survey results that provide insights into social issues, politics, sports, entertainment, the environment, and other topics.

http://www.kahs.org
The Web site for the Korean American Historical Society contains links to information on a century of Korean immigration to the United States, from 1903 to 2003.

http://www.lindasuepark.com
Author Linda Sue Park's official Web site contains her blog, a list of her favorite books as an adult and as a child, a biography, and trivia quizzes.

http://www.pih.org
The Web site for Partners in Health contains information on the organization's mission and its current efforts to improve the health of poor people around the world.

http://www.usc.edu/libraries/collections/korean_american
The University of Southern California maintains the Korean-American Digital Archive, which contains links to documents, photographs, and oral histories of people from the Korean-American community.

Dosan Ahn (1878–1938): Born in today's South Pyongan, North Korea, Ahn came to the United States in 1902 and became a leader in the Korean-American community. The educator and activist established the Mutual Assistance Society (which became the Korean National Association) to represent Koreans living outside Korea and work for Korean independence during the Japanese occupation. A memorial park dedicated in 1973 to the Korean nationalist leader is in Seoul.

Philip Ahn (1905–1978): Born in Los Angeles, Ahn was a television and film character actor who

Violin virtuoso Sarah Chang has collaborated with such major orchestras as the New York Philharmonic, the Philadelphia Orchestra, the Berlin Philharmonic, and the London Symphony.

played Chinese and Japanese roles, as well as Korean ones. He worked from the mid-1930s until the early 1970s, during a time when few Asian actors were in the business. In 1984 Ahn was honored for his contributions to the motion picture industry with a star on the Hollywood Walk of Fame.

Sarah Chang (1980–): Born in Philadelphia, Pennsylvania, Chang began playing violin at age four. A child prodigy, she first performed with major orchestras when she was eight years old. In 2006 *Newsweek* magazine included her in its 20 Top Women on Leadership, and the World Economic Forum honored her as a Young Global Leader for 2008.

Frank Cho (1971–): Born in Seoul, Korea, and raised in Beltsville, Maryland, Cho is a cartoon strip artist who went from drawing for the student newspaper at his college, the University of Maryland, to publishing a professionally syndicated strip called Liberty Meadows. He has also created artwork for Marvel Comics' *The New Avengers*, *The Mighty Avengers*, and *Hulk*.

Herbert Choy (1916–2004): Born in Makaweli, Hawaii, Choy was the first person of Korean heritage granted the right to practice law in the United States. In 1971 he was appointed to the U.S. Court of Appeals for the Ninth Circuit, becoming the first Asian American to serve as a U.S. federal judge.

Jamie Chung (1983–): Born in San Francisco, California, Chung got her start as an actress on the MTV reality show *The Real World: San Diego*. She has had parts on other television programs and starred in the 2008 ABC Family show *Samurai Girl*.

Joe Hahn (1977–): Born in Glendale, California, Hahn is a founder and Grammy Award–winning artist of the alternative rock band Linkin Park. He serves as the band's DJ and turntablist and as video director for many of the group's music videos.

Philip Jaisohn (1864–1951): Born in Boseong, Korea, Jaisohn came to the United States as a refugee after participating in a failed coup in 1884. He was the first Korean to become a naturalized American citizen, in 1890, and the first to receive a U.S. medical degree, in 1892. He worked in Korea and the United States to help his homeland gain independence as a democracy. In 2008 the Korean Consulate in Washington, D.C., unveiled a statue in his honor.

Jay Kim (1939–): Born in Seoul, Korea, Kim is the first Korean-American member of the U.S. Congress. He became a member of the House of Representatives in 1993, representing the 41st District of California, and served until January 1999.

Michael Kim (1964–): Born in Fulton, Missouri, Kim is an anchor for the ESPN sports news television shows *SportsCenter* and *ESPNEWS*. He has been recognized with a local Emmy Award for sports reporting.

Chang-Rae Lee (1965–): Born in Korea, Lee is the director of creative writing at Princeton University. His first book, *Native Speaker*, was published in 1995 and was a winner of the PEN/Hemingway Award.

Sammy Lee (1920–): Born in Fresno, California, Lee was a platform diver and the first Asian American to win an Olympic gold medal for the United States, in 1948. He repeated his gold medal in 1952. After retiring from competitive diving, he worked as a physician and coached divers. In 1990 Le was inducted into the U.S. Olympic Hall of Fame.

Richard Park, who is the second Korean-born person to play in the National Hockey League, plays right wing for the New York Islanders.

Jim Paek (1967–): Born in Seoul, South Korea, Paek was the first Korean-born player in the National Hockey League (NHL). The first Korean to have his name engraved on the Stanley Cup (the NHL championship trophy), he has been recognized by the Hockey Hall of Fame.

Richard Park (1976–): Born in Seoul, South Korea, Park came to the United States with his family when he was three years old. He has played on minor league hockey teams and in the National Hockey League with the Pittsburgh Penguins, Philadelphia Flyers, and New York Islanders, among others. He is the second Korean-born person to play in the NHL.

Aaron Yoo (1979–): Born in East Brunswick, New Jersey, Yoo is an actor who has appeared in television and motion pictures. His films include *American Pastime* (2007), *Disturbia* (2007), and *Nick and Norah's Infinite Playlist* (2008).

Other Successful Korean Americans

INDEX

PICTURE CREDITS

ABOUT THE AUTHOR

Gail Snyder is a freelance writer and advertising copywriter who has written numerous books for young readers. She lives in Chalfont, Pennsylvania, with her husband, Hal, daughter Ashley and cat, Lucky. She is a second-generation Russian American.